Fall Walk

To the Original Master, who created the trees, leaves, and children I love and enjoy so much.

Printed in China by Toppan

Paperback Edition
25 24   5 4 3

Text © 2019 Virginia Brimhall Snow
Illustrations © 2019 Virginia Brimhall Snow

Published by
Gibbs Smith
P.O. Box 667
Layton, Utah 84041

1.800.835.4993 orders
www.gibbs-smith.com

Designed by Andrew Brozyna
Gibbs Smith books are printed on either recycled, 100% post-consumer waste, FSC-certified papers or on paper produced from sustainable PEFC-certified forest/controlled wood source. Learn more at www.pefc.org.

Library of Congress Cataloging-in-Publication Data

Snow, Virginia Brimhall.
 Fall walk / Virginia Brimhall Snow. — 1st ed.
   p. cm.
 ISBN 978-1-4236-3261-0 (hardcover)
 ISBN 978-1-4236-5391-2 (paperback)
 1. Leaves—Morphology—Juvenile literature.
 2. Leaves—Color—Juvenile
literature. 3. Fall foliage—Juvenile literature. I. Title.
 QK649.S66 2013
 575.5'7—dc23
                                    2012051243

Fall Walk

VIRGINIA BRIMHALL SNOW

GIBBS SMITH
TO ENRICH AND INSPIRE HUMANKIND

POPLAR

I went for a walk in
the leaves today.

They rustled and crunched
as I kicked them away.

WILLOW

FLOWERING PLUM

COTTONWOOD

Red, orange, yellow,
purple and brown,

They flew into the air
and then fluttered down.

SYCAMORE

FLOWERING PEAR

My grammy told me
the name of each one,

Remembering was hard,
but I still had fun.

WALNUT

I twirled and ran and
jumped in a pile,

Scattering the leaves
made Grammy smile.

RUSSIAN OLIVE

MULBERRY

"See these leaves,
they're mulberry,

And this big red one
is a chokecherry."

CANADA RED CHOKECHERRY

SWEET GUM

As I looked closer,
I saw red, gold, and green,

With veins edge-to-edge
and small ones between.

HONEY LOCUST

Wind lifted leaves up and
whirled them around,

I joined in their dance 'til
they fell to the ground.

SASSAFRAS

OAK

BIRCH

Fall colors on the mountain
glowed in the sun

From the autumn leaves,
their work almost done.

MAPLE

ASPEN

The maple leaf was
all spiky and red.

I held round aspen leaves
that turn yellow when dead.

PEACH

Leaves from the peach tree
were pointed and gold.

I told my grammy,
"There are too many to hold!"

HAWTHORN

ELM

So we pulled out a bag
at the end of the day,

And Grammy told me
as we started away,

GOLDEN RAIN TREE

PECAN

"Let's take a few home
to press in a book.

When you want to remember,
open and look."

GINKGO

Can you match the leaf to the tree that it comes from?
To check your answers, look back through the book.

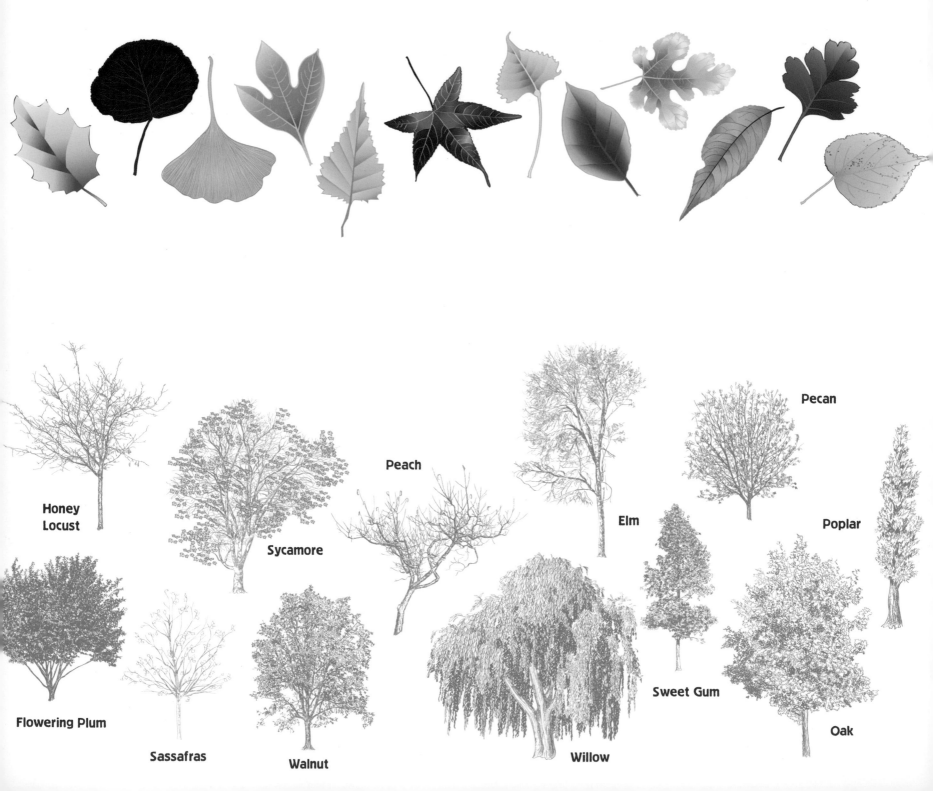

Honey
Locust

Sycamore

Peach

Elm

Pecan

Poplar

Flowering Plum

Sassafras

Walnut

Willow

Sweet Gum

Oak

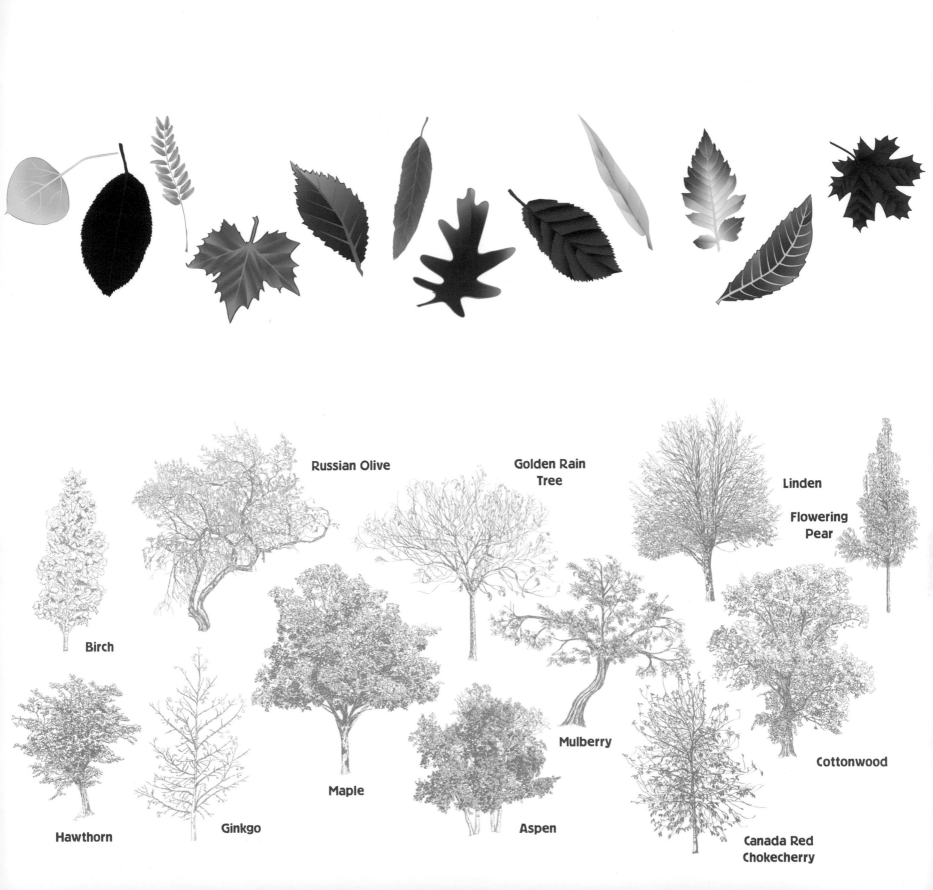

Russian Olive

Golden Rain
Tree

Linden

Flowering
Pear

Birch

Mulberry

Cottonwood

Hawthorn

Ginkgo

Maple

Aspen

Canada Red
Chokecherry

HOW TO PRESS LEAVES

YOU WILL NEED:

- Leaves that are still soft, not dry and crunchy

- A few large books (that dictionary you never use is perfect)

- A few blank papers

Prepare a place where the leaves can dry undisturbed for a few days.

Put down a book, a paper, and then some of your leaves. It's best if the leaves don't touch each other. Cover them with a paper and stack a book on top. Continue building the stack with the paper, leaf, paper, and book sequence. Finish by placing a couple of really thick books on top.

In a few days, your leaves will be pressed.

LEAF RUBBING

YOU WILL NEED:

- Soft or pressed leaves in a variety of shapes

- Crayons without their wrappers

- Paper

Place a leaf on a hard surface vein side up. Cover it with paper. With the side of the crayon, rub across the paper over the leaf and watch the outline and veins appear. Firm pressure with a bright crayon gives the best results.

Try making your very own leaf book.

Making a festive fall table covering is fun. Use a large piece of butcher paper and let your friends help you with lots of colors and different leaf shapes.

TREE TRIVIA

1. The sassafras tree has more than one shape of leaf on the same tree.

2. Maple syrup is made by drilling a hole in the trunk of a sugar maple tree and collecting the sap (tree blood). The sap is then condensed until it becomes maple syrup.

3. The world's largest living organism is a grove of aspen trees in Utah, USA, named Pando.

4. Silk is made by silkworms that eat white mulberry leaves.

5. Fruit growers trim their trees so the fruit will grow bigger and better.

6. Chlorophyll is the stuff in leaves that makes them green. It hides the yellow and orange colors that are also there. When autumn comes, the tree stops making chlorophyll and we see the beautiful colors.

7. Maple tree seeds whirl in the air like helicopters when they fall.

8. Willow bark contains a chemical that is similar to aspirin, so it is used to relieve headache and muscle pain.

9. Trees take in carbon dioxide through their leaves and give off oxygen.

10. Sir Isaac Newton discovered the law of gravity while sitting under an apple tree.